BATIK *Art and Craft*

BATIK
Art and Craft

Nik Krevitsky

An Art Horizons Book

Van Nostrand Reinhold Company
New York Cincinnati Toronto London Melbourne

*Frontispiece: Traditional Indian figurative
batik; courtesy, Standard Oil Co. (N. J.)*

Van Nostrand Reinhold Company Regional Offices:
New York   Cincinnati   Chicago   Millbrae   Dallas

Van Nostrand Reinhold Company International Offices:
London   Toronto   Melbourne

Library of Congress Catalog Card Number 64-13647
ISBN 0-442-24539-4

Printed in England by Jolly and Barber Ltd, Rugby,
Warwickshire.

Published by Van Nostrand Reinhold Company
A division of Litton Educational Publishing, Inc.
450 West 33rd Street, New York, N.Y. 10001

Published simultaneously in Canada by
Van Nostrand Reinhold Ltd.

16 15 14 13 12 11 10 9 8 7

CONTENTS

FOREWORD

The question "Batik, what's that?" is one reason for writing this book. When the last popular book on the subject was published in 1919 this craft was at the height of its vogue. At that time batik and other crafts kept decorative artists busy producing laboriously detailed ornamentation for the age of opulence. Since then, a great depression, another world war, mechanization, automation, electronic marvels, space travel, and other realities of the twentieth century have affected the American attitude toward arts, crafts, and the individual.

During recent decades we have found ourselves searching for personal identity and values in a world that seems to have little room for them. The vast expansion of technical information and know-how and the population explosion impinge on our relationships to each other as individuals and to the world. The need for self-identity has never been greater, and the arts and crafts provide one outstanding means of making contact with the creative potential that lies within all of us. The need to produce and own handmade objects is in part a reaction against the machine-dominated aspect of almost everything we see or touch and also a search for our own worth as human beings. There is little doubt that handcrafts fashioned with love and hard work have come into new importance because they impart a feeling of great pride and joy in knowing that the work was conceived and done by an individual, not a machine.

Batik has come back, revitalized and invigorated. It is a technique that allows, simply and effectively, the production of a personal statement, a work of art.

When I was asked to write a basic informative book on batik, I accepted because I was aware that no recent examples or ideas had been assembled as a guide. Research into the subject has reinforced my confidence in the craft as an important and vital activity of man. My reward has been great because this book may serve as an answer to "Batik, what's that?" and as a guide to those who wish to express their individuality through a highly rewarding medium. It is my sincere hope that the following chapters will permit the reader an intimate contact with this fine art form and impart some of the joy I have had in learning about batik and practicing it.

Nik Krevitsky

INTRODUCTION

The art of batik has been known for centuries, but its origin, probably thousands of years ago, is still obscure. Briefly, batik is a resist technique for producing designs on fabrics. The process, in simplified form, follows these general steps: Selected areas of the fabric are blocked out by brushing melted wax or a special paste over them. After the wax is applied, the fabric is dyed by brushing dye over it or by dipping it into a dye bath. The waxed areas, repelling the dye, remain the original color of the fabric. To achieve more intricate designs with further combinations and overlays of color the waxing and dyeing process is repeated.

While a simple batik can be made by using only one dye color, the usual number is two or three. Some batik artists use up to 20 separate waxing and dyeing steps to achieve highly intricate designs. Since the colors are dyed one on top of the other—except where areas of the fabric are waxed out—they combine to produce new colors. The batik craftsman must be aware of the basic facts of color mixing to take advantage of this fact.

After the final dyeing, the wax is removed from the fabric with heat or solvents or by scraping. The decorated fabric is then ready for use as intended: for a wall hanging, a room divider, or as material for a variety of garments.

The Malaysian word *batik* is the term most commonly applied to this resist process, since it is in Java that this art form was most extensively developed and has been continually practiced on a large scale. Batik continues to be a major industry in Java, and evidence derived from the ancient decorative arts of that country indicates that it has changed little from the time, centuries ago, when it was first practiced there. From Java batik was introduced to Europe by Dutch traders, who first imported batiks to Holland in the middle of the seventeenth century. Although batik is still practiced in the traditional way in the Far East, its time-consuming method makes the true process prohibitive to most Westerners.

The modern Western approach to batik is quite different from the traditional Javanese method. It tends to be freer, bolder, and more direct and spontaneous in concept and actual production. Many contemporary artists, both Eastern and Western, think of batiking as they do of painting—as a means for developing an individual, unique work of art. Westerners also use batik to decorate fabrics. Many of the currently popular fabric designs are batik inspired or reproduced from batiks themselves. The reproduced prints can duplicate exactly the pattern of an original, but they lack the uniqueness of the handmade article. In addition, the wearer is deprived of the pleasure of showing off an original design, perhaps his own.

Contemporary batik artists simplify the traditional procedure in many ways. To prepare the fabric, they merely wash it to remove sizing or other filler in order to allow for shrinkage, and to remove excess dye if colored fabric is being used. Wax is applied with brushes, and commercial dyes are used instead of home-made natural dyes. These simplifications make it possible for almost anyone—child, adult beginner, or professional—to create a work of art using the batik technique.

Many new applications of batik are emerging as new and different media are being explored by science. The modern chemical industries have invented new wax formulas and improved dyes. Fabrics are still undergoing the revolution initiated by the invention of synthetics. These developments will naturally lead to new frontiers in batik. The possibilities of this age-old technique are far from being exhausted; there are many opportunities for innovation.

1. TRADITIONAL BATIK METHODS

Batik probably originated in the East, and traditional methods of batiking, sometimes using natural dyes, are still practiced there in some places. The following sections present two age-old methods of resist printing: the Javanese wax resist and the paste resist techniques. Both methods are laborious and slow, and do not lend themselves to the more spontaneous creative needs of the modern artist and craftsman. However, the methods are of great interest, and by following the photographic sequences in this chapter, the student, adult beginner, or professional will develop an awareness of how a beautiful art technique has been gracefully maintained through traditional practice. It is not suggested that the general reader undertake the tedious recapitulation of either of these methods. Only the researcher, museum curator, or art historian might need to recreate the highly technical sequences.

JAVANESE WAX RESIST

Although the wax resist method of dyeing fabrics has been practiced in India, China, and throughout the Far East, the Javanese batik is of the greatest interest, primarily because of the elegance of design and the still current importance of its production in the life and economy of the country. Batiks have been made continuously in Java since the technique was introduced from either Persia or India, probably in the 12th century. Java is also the one place where the technique is still widely practiced, in some areas much as it was hundreds of years ago.

There are two major types of Javanese batik: the *tulis*, or hand drawn, and the *tjap* printed. The tulis batiks are the finest examples of batik work. Their designs are entirely drawn or painted in wax by hand with a tool known as the *tjanting*. A two-yard-long tulis may take from 30 to 50 days to produce, with about 15 days being devoted to waxing in the design.

Tulis batiks, because of the time spent producing them and the intricacy of design permitted by hand waxing, have always been expensive. They were formerly worn only by the nobility and very wealthy Javanese. Today they are worn not only as dress but are popular with Westerners as decoration.

Tjap, or stamp waxed, batiks are handsome, but the quality of their designs is limited by the mechanical aspect of their production. Tjap patterns are exactly repeated geometric forms or stylized natural shapes. The tjap batik may be produced far more rapidly than the tulis, and therefore costs much less. Most of the 40,000,000 yards of fabric batiked each year are done with the tjap technique.

PASTE RESIST

Paste resist is probably the oldest form of batik. It was widely practiced throughout the Middle and Far East and is still done in Japan, Indonesia, India, Africa, and Okinawa .

There are various kinds of paste resists, but combinations of rice and other flours are most common. The rice and bran flour mixture widely used in Japan is combined with small amounts of powdered zinc sulphate and salt and cooked to make a transparent cream, which is stirred until cool.

Paste may be applied in numerous ways, including brushing freehand or with stencils, dabbing with the fingers, and squeezing it through a stiff paper tube. The tube, which resembles a pastry tube both in appearance and use, is filled and rolled from the top to force the paste through the small open end.

The dye in paste resist batiks is usually applied to only one surface. It is prepared by mixing powdered dye with a gum solution, which gives it a stiff consistency and prevents the spreading inevitable with more watery substances. The dye solution is used cold. Because the fabric is not immersed, various colors may be applied in different areas—as long as the areas are separated by paste or distance. The final dye step usually consists of brushing a dark dye over the whole piece of cloth.

A steam bath is used to set the dye. Several lengths of fabric are steamed together. Each length is separated by many sheets of newspaper and then all are rolled together. This roll is then rolled in more sheets of paper and the ends folded and tied. The batch is covered with a heavy cloth and hung in a steam closet. The fabric is steamed thoroughly for at least an hour; heavy fabrics require more time.

After the fabric is removed from the steam bath, it is washed in clear, cold water and rinsed several times until the paste is completely removed. After it is dry, the fabric is ironed and the process is complete.

Squeezing off the oil. The fabric is then boiled in water to separate out oil not absorbed by the fibers. Next, it is beaten with wooden paddles to make it supple and to realign the weave, and starched to prevent the wax from running.

Preparing the fabric. Before any of the laborious design application is begun, the fabric—usually white cotton cambric—is carefully treated. First it is washed in hot water to pre-shrink it and to remove any filler, thus making it pliable. It is then steeped in coconut oil or castor oil so that the fibers will accept the dye more readily. In this illustration the fabric is being inspected for suppleness.

Weighing the ingredients for the resist. Although the proportions are well-guarded secrets of the various factories, the wax resist usually consists of combinations of paraffin, beeswax, resin, varnish gums, and tallow. These come from distant parts of the globe, the beeswax being imported from America. The ingredients are melted together and cast into blocks.

Photos courtesy Standard Oil Co. (N. J.)

First outline waxing of the batik.
The design has already been carefully
sketched in with charcoal. The young
woman follows the charcoal drawing
precisely, depositing a fine line of wax
with the tjanting. She then turns the
fabric over and waxes the back to
adequately protect the fabric from the
dye when it is immersed in the dye bath.

To prepare the day's supply of wax,
the batiker flakes pieces from a block
of wax and puts them into an iron pot
set on a charcoal burner. The wax is kept
in a liquid state throughout the day by
continually stoking the burner.

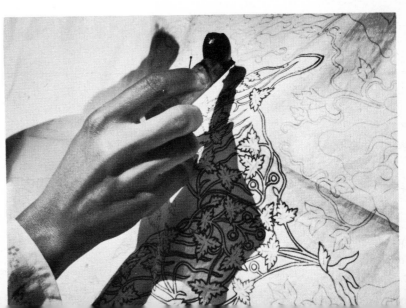

Detail showing use of the tjanting.
This technique is known as the tulis, or
hand drawing, method of batiking.

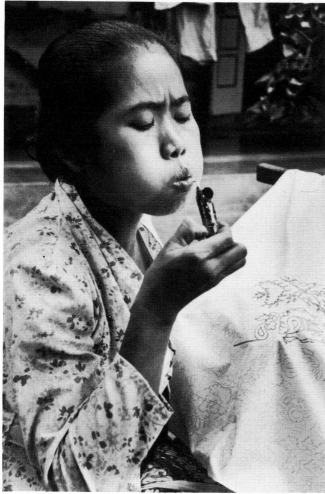

To maintain an even flow of wax, the craftsman periodically blows into the spout of the tjanting to clear it. The tjanting is filled by being dipped into the pot of melted wax. The batik artist sits on the ground and works on a fabric hanging from a bamboo frame.

A variety of tjantings showing single and multiple spouts. The multiple-spouted tjantings deposit parallel lines or dots. Some spouts are so narrow that they leave a wax line only 1/25 inch thick. The bowl of a tjanting is copper or bronze, both good conductors of heat, and is tapered at the top to help retain the heat. The spout is also carefully tapered from bowl end to tip for proper flow of the hot wax.

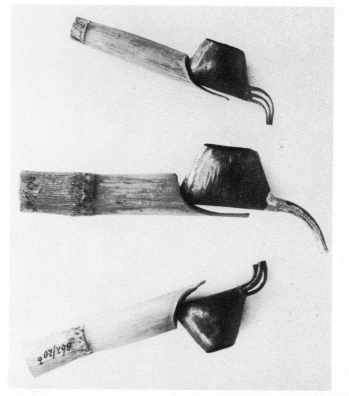

Second waxing of the fabric. Areas that are to remain white or indigo are covered by another coat of wax. The second waxing, like the first, must be done on both sides of the fabric. The fabric is then immersed in the second dye, usually a reddish brown. The uncovered white areas dye reddish brown, and the unwaxed indigo areas turn a rich deep brown.

After the first application of wax, the batik receives its first dye, usually indigo blue. As soon as the fabrics are pulled out of the dye vat, they are hung straight so that the wax does not crack and the dye remains even. When the fabric is dry, the first wax design—or parts of it—is scraped off. The underlying parts, which have been protected by the wax, are white.

Preparing sago bark for making reddish-brown dyes. The bark is chopped into small pieces and soaked with a mordant to make the second color of the traditional brown and blue Javanese batik.

Batik being dipped in the second dye bath,
the reddish-brown dye made from the
bark of the sago tree of Borneo. The tub
is large enough to allow the fabric to be
completely immersed and agitated in
the bath.

Drying batiks after the second, and final,
application of dye. This step is followed
by boiling the fabric in water to remove
the wax. The wax residue is salvaged
to be mixed with fresh wax for later use.

Finished batiks hanging in the sun to dry
after the wax has been boiled away
in water.

One of the most intricate traditional
*Djogja batiks, made by the process
previously described. This pattern,
which required six months to complete,
is called* sruni *after a local flower.
The* sruni *batiks are used as sarongs and
reserved for formal functions.*

Photos courtesy Republic of Indonesia

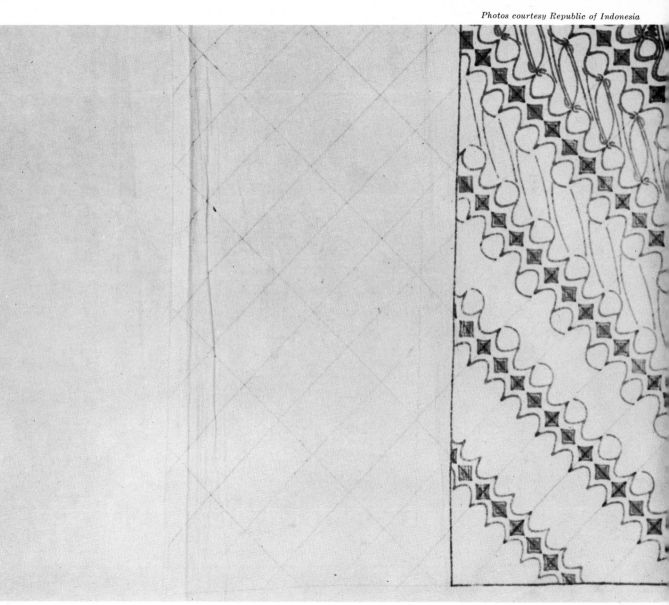

1. *The prepared fabric after washing, oiling, boiling, beating, and soaking in thin starch*

2. *Basic outline in charcoal of the geometric design*

3. *The first outlining in wax, done with the tjanting*

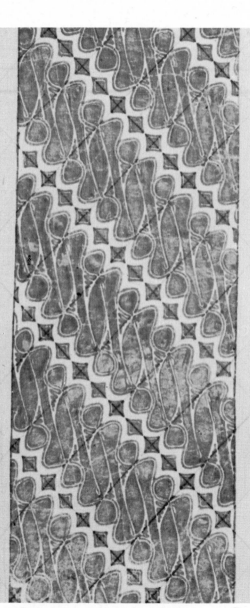

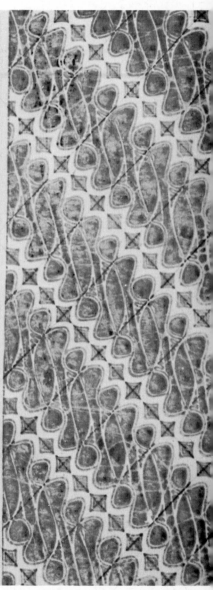

4. *Reverse side of the fabric, showing its coat of wax*

5. *Large areas not to be dyed the first color have been waxed*

6. *Reverse side, showing same treatment*

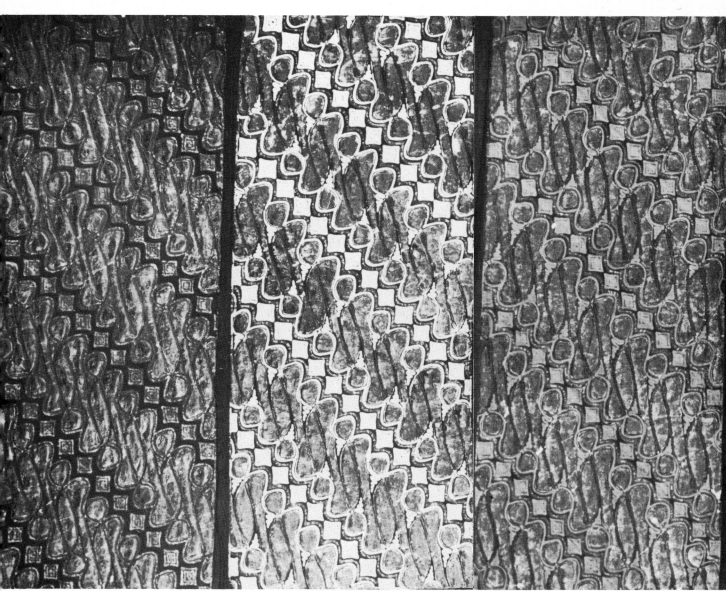

7. *First dyeing, in indigo*

8. *Areas to be dyed the second color have been scraped and wax applied to those that are to remain indigo*

9. *Second dyeing, in reddish-brown*

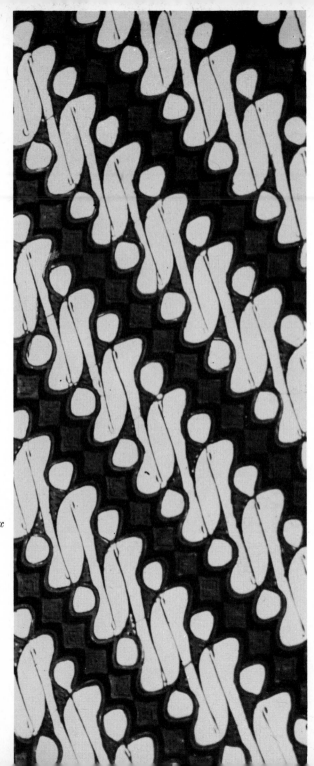

*10. The finished batik, after it has been
     washed in hot water to remove the wax*

Tjap waxing can be done in a fraction of the time that it takes to trace a design with the tjanting. One man may produce as many as 20 tjap batiks in a single day, while it ordinarily takes several women weeks to complete one hand-waxed work. The tjap stamp is made of metal. The lines of the design are formed by thin strips of copper and the dots by short stumps of wire. These are soldered to a solid copper base with an attached iron handle.
The artisan presses the tjap onto a pad saturated with molten wax and then applies it to the cloth. This must be done on both sides of the fabric, and matching the design requires considerable skill.

Photos courtesy Standard Oil Co. (N. J.)

Stamp printing with the tjap, a tool devised for accelerating the production of batiks. Tjap stamping was introduced into Java in 1850 from Madras, India, where it had been used extensively since the 15th century. Stamping is done almost exclusively by men, whereas women do the meticulous work of hand drawing in wax with the tjanting.

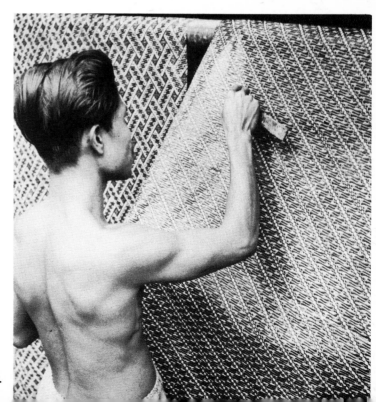

Scraping the tjap printed batik after the first dyeing. Between dye immersions, areas to be exposed for subsequent colors are scraped with a smooth wooden stick. The stick is used for scraping hand-waxed as well as tjap-printed batiks.

Most of the paste is applied freehand, using a tube, brush, or—as illustrated here—the fingers. Delicate outlines may be laid in using the tube and the interior of the form gently patted in with the fingers. The paste resist design can be clearly seen to the right of the artisan's arm.

Applying the paste. The batiker sits in front of the fabric, which is stretched by bamboo braces and suspended between small wooden horses. Here she is making small details by squeezing paste through a tube.

Drying the fabric. After each application of paste or dye, the fabric must be thoroughly dried. Here several strips are hung across the room. As the fabric dries it becomes lighter and the bamboo sticks become straighter as the weight diminishes. Thus, because of the flexibility of the bamboo, the fabric remains taut.

2. CONTEMPORARY BATIK TECHNIQUES

Dyeing by Immersion

Although many variations of the basic batik technique are possible, a simplified version of the traditional Javanese process will be demonstrated first. This method involves applying wax to the fabric with brushes and dyeing by immersion.

Once this technique is mastered, one may go on to its variations: brushing dyes directly onto the fabric, and using the tjanting.

MATERIALS

No unusual materials or equipment are required for first experiments in batik. Most of the items listed below are ordinarily available in the kitchen or classroom.

FABRICS

Closely woven, thin fabrics are best for batik. Sheer cottons and silks are excellent. Used fabrics such as worn sheets work well, especially for preliminary experiments. Avoid fabrics treated with water repellents—such as drip-dry fabrics; they contain resins which may cause difficulties in dyeing. Some synthetic fabrics, such as orlon and nylon, can be used for making batiks, but only with dyes specially formulated for them. Heavier fabrics, such as the heavier cottons and silks or linens, can be used successfully in batik; however, since wax penetrates them less readily, they will require waxing on both sides to prevent the dye from penetrating the waxed areas from the underside. Heavier fabrics may also require greater quantities of water and more dye stuff, since the weight of the fabric exhausts more of the dye from the bath and absorbs more of the liquid. Insufficient dye can cause irregular coloring.

DYES

Many of the household dyes commonly available in drug and variety stores are satisfactory. Do not use dyes that require boiling the fabric, as this will melt the wax. Dyes should be of a type that can be used in lukewarm water. Be sure that the dye used is compatible with the fabric to be batiked—and follow directions carefully.

Colored waterproof inks are recommended for accents. Both dyes and waterproof inks can be used when color is applied to the fabric by brushing rather than by immersion. Felt-tip pens containing strong alcohol dyes provide a means of making accents conveniently.

WAX

Ordinary paraffin is adequate and inexpensive. A slight addition of beeswax to the paraffin will provide a more flexible medium. The ideal resist medium contains mostly beeswax; it is very flexible and will hold up under immersion in warmer dye baths. Beeswax is, however, very expensive—unless a local beekeeper can provide it in its unrefined state.

TOOLS

Brushes are the only tools needed for the basic wax and dye technique. An assortment of expendable, inexpensive brushes should be on hand. Bristle brushes are good for painting large areas or making wide strokes. Soft brushes, such as the inexpensive Japanese ink brushes, are useful for small areas and thin lines. Do not use fine watercolor brushes. They work very well, but they are expensive and difficult to clean thoroughly once they have been dipped in hot wax. Wax stiffened brushes become flexible again when they are dipped in hot wax. Wax may be removed from brushes with mineral solvents.

Improvised implements for applying wax can provide a variety of unusual textural effects. Objects used in stamp printing—such as pieces of wood, corks, sponge fragments, etc.—can be dipped in hot wax and applied to the fabric. A syringe or plastic dispenser can be used for squirting wax onto the fabric for spontaneous lines and patterns.

SPECIAL EQUIPMENT

Electric plate for heating the wax container. (If wax is heated over an open flame, an asbestos mat should be used)
Double boiler or tin can (placed in a pan of water) in which to heat the wax
Electric iron for removing the wax from the fabric
Waxed paper, newsprint, newspaper
Large glass, copper, or enamel container in which to dye the fabric
Rubber gloves
Stirring sticks
Plastic clothesline and clothespins
Acetic acid for fixing the dye (household vinegar will do)
Solvents for removing the wax (e.g., mineral spirits, commercial cleaning fluids, gasoline, kerosene)

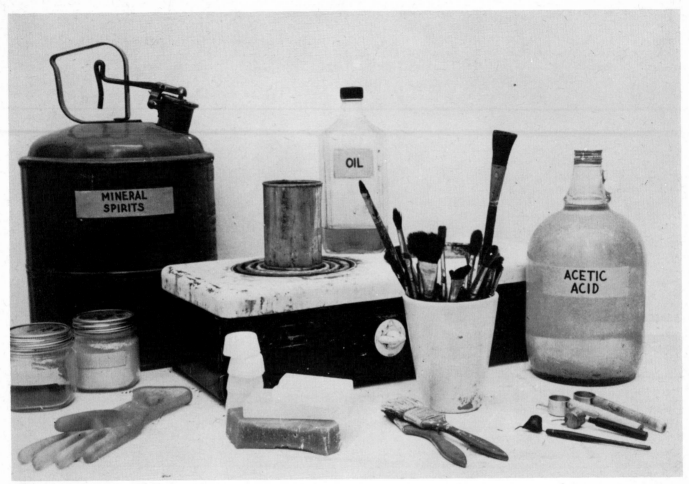

Basic equipment for beginning experiments in batik. From left to right: solvent for final cleaning, jars of dyes, rubber gloves, electric plate and tin can for heating wax, oil for preliminary fabric rinse, paraffin and beeswax, assorted brushes, acetic acid for setting dyes, assorted tjantings.

1. Fabric showing preliminary drawing and first waxing covering areas to remain white

Photos by Peter Balestrero

PREPARING THE FABRIC

It is advisable to wash and press the fabric in preparation for the waxing. Washing will remove any filler from the fabric and prevent later shrinkage during the dyeings. Next, apply a thin starch solution to the fabric and press it. Starching permits a smooth application of the wax and prevents edges of the wax from bleeding during the waxing process.

DRAWING THE DESIGN

Although one may begin by working spontaneously on the fabric without a preliminary design in mind, it is helpful to work from a drawing or plan. If one is able to visualize the additive aspect of the technique, a complete color sketch might be of considerable help in the actual making of the batik.

The easiest method—which was used in the accompanying demonstration—is to draw with charcoal the areas to be reserved on the fabric in the first waxing. Charcoal will wash out in the many dippings and rinsings of the fabric. Other sketching materials, such as

2. First dyeing (yellow). Waxed areas have resisted the dye

pencil, are less likely to wash out.
A design may be transferred from an
original drawing by using carbon paper
or by using a pricking wheel, which
produces a delicate pinpoint line on
the fabric.

FIRST WAXING

Brush melted wax onto the fabric in
lines or areas to be reserved. This will
protect those areas which are to remain
the original color of the fabric (white, in
the accompanying demonstration). It is
important to plan this and subsequent
waxing steps in advance. At no later
stage, once a dyeing is done, may one
retrieve a color unless controlled
bleaching is possible.

Waxing may be done in several ways.
If it is desirable to work with the fabric
in a horizontal position, place it on a flat
surface protected with waxed paper or
other smooth, non-absorbent material.
For greater control, the fabric may be
stretched over an improvised frame, such
as a canvas stretcher or large wooden
picture frame, and tacked down with push

3. Second waxing covering areas to remain yellow

pins. If the fabric is larger than the frame, it can be moved over the frame and waxed one section at a time.

If the worker prefers to see the entire surface all at once, a vertical frame, such as a curtain stretcher, is recommended. However, the vertical position is awkward and uncomfortable for the batik technique because of the flow of the wax on the brush or other tools used. For brushing in large areas, however, the vertical position works very well. The wax must be kept hot enough to penetrate the fabric immediately upon contact. When the wax begins to dry on the surface of the fabric, it is time to reheat it.

After the first waxing, inspect the fabric for penetration of the wax. If the fabric is heavy, it may be necessary to apply wax over the same areas on the reverse side. Thin fabrics such as silk seldom require double waxing.

FIRST DYEING

It is advisable to make the first color the lightest one used, and to conceive the design as one in which colors add to

4. Second dyeing (red). The red combines with the yellow where the design is exposed to the dye

each other, as overlays, to build up the final design. Everything dyed the first color will influence the subsequent colors to some extent. In the accompanying demonstration the first color is yellow.

Mix the dye according to directions. Most dyes recommend the following: 1) dilution with hot water, 2) straining to remove any undiluted particles, 3) addition of enough water to comfortably cover the fabric, 4) wetting the fabric before immersion in the dye, 5) constant stirring for even application, 6) careful removal from the dye bath, 7) rinsing in clear water to remove the excess dye, and hanging to dry.

The success of a batik depends to a large extent upon following carefully the dyeing procedure. As mentioned earlier, since batik must be done with cool, or no more than tepid, dye baths, the dyes which require boiling must be avoided. Hot water would melt the wax and cold water tends to make the wax too brittle. Some dyes, especially those for silk, require boiling *before* use, even though they take well when applied warm to the

5. *Third waxing, covering areas to remain the color of the second dyeing*

fabric. To control the temperature, it is well to have a thermometer to test the heat. Paraffin melts at a lower degree than beeswax. If paraffin is used, the temperature of the dye bath should be kept below 90° F. Pure beeswax can be exposed to a heat of 110° F. without melting.

The amount of water necessary depends upon the fabric to be dyed. But one must always have at least enough to cover the fabric easily and to fill a container large enough to permit constant stirring. The fabric should literally swim in the dye. To help the color go on evenly and easily, a pure soap may be added to the dye bath. One tablespoon of powdered soap added to the average dye bath is enough. For silk, an olive oil soap, like castile, adds a fine lustre to the dye. Soap powder can also be added to the final clear rinses to help set the dye.

Dye becomes streaked if applied to dry fabrics. Therefore the fabric should first be thoroughly and evenly wet by careful immersion in lukewarm water. Since the batik fabric has already been

6. Third dyeing (chestnut brown)

prepared by washing and drying before the first application of wax, there is no need to follow dye directions about removing filler from new fabric. Because the dyeing, to be successful, requires moving the fabric about in the bath with a dye-stick or with one's hands (protected by rubber gloves), it is not convenient to dye isolated areas of batik by immersing. Designs requiring this can be more easily dyed by brushing dye onto the fabric, as demonstrated in the next section.

For good, even dyeing, every part of the fabric must be equally exposed to the action of the dye. This is achieved by stirring, turning, and lifting the fabric. Allowing the fabric to remain in the bath in one position can result in a variety of accidental effects. Always remember that colors will appear brighter and darker when the fabric is wet. Therefore, the craftsman is advised to allow the fabric to remain in the dye longer than the color desired.

After the dye is applied, the fabric should be rinsed carefully to remove the

7. *Fourth waxing, covering areas to remain brown and leaving exposed those areas to be dyed the final, and darkest, color—black*

excess dye. Blot the fabric before hanging it to dry to prevent streaking and running. Wringing is not recommended. To dry the fabric, hang it carefully from one side (not doubled over) with clothespins on a plastic clothesline.

SECOND WAXING

When the fabric is completely dry after the first dyeing it is ready for the second reserving of wax. This application of wax will cover those areas which are to remain the color of the first dye. Wax is again applied, as previously, with careful inspection of the reverse side of the fabric.

DYEING THE SECOND COLOR

The fabric is then dipped into the second color (in the accompanying demonstration, red), following the procedure outlined for the first dyeing. The action of the red over the yellow creates an orange hue. The second color is also slightly darkened by combination with the first.

8. Fourth dyeing in black

THIRD WAXING

After the fabric has been dried for the second time, areas to remain the color of the second dye are covered with wax as before. At this stage the fabric has wax over the white, yellow, and orange areas. The remaining, unwaxed areas will be dyed the next color—chestnut brown.

DYEING THE THIRD COLOR

The fabric is immersed in the third color (in the demonstration, chestnut brown), following the usual procedure. The chestnut brown dye combines with the second color to produce a rich, warm brown.

FOURTH WAXING AND FINAL DYEING

After the fabric is dry following the third dyeing, areas to remain brown are waxed out. The remaining exposed areas will be dyed the final, darkest color—in this case, black.

FINISHING THE BATIK

The fabric after final dyeing is finished by removal of all the wax. This is done

9. Batik with all the wax removed

by pressing it with a hot iron. Place several sheets of newspaper over the ironing surface and cover them with plain newsprint. Lay the fabric on this, and cover it with newsprint and newspaper, in that order. Press with sufficient heat to melt the wax out of the fabric. The ironing must be done several times, and an adequate supply of absorbent paper, paper towels, or old cloth should be available to simplify this procedure.

Fabric may also be dipped in a vat of gasoline, kerosene, or other inexpensive solvent which will dissolve the wax. This treatment removes the wax more thoroughly than does the ironing, but special precautions must be taken when working with flammable and sometimes toxic solutions.

Unless very strong, special batik dyes have been used, it is unwise to wash the finished article; therefore dry cleaning is recommended. An excellent procedure for fixing the dye is to steam it with an acetic acid solution (such as white household vinegar). A simple method for doing this is to cover the finished batik with a cloth saturated with the solution and press it with the iron.

Two-color batik by junior high school student

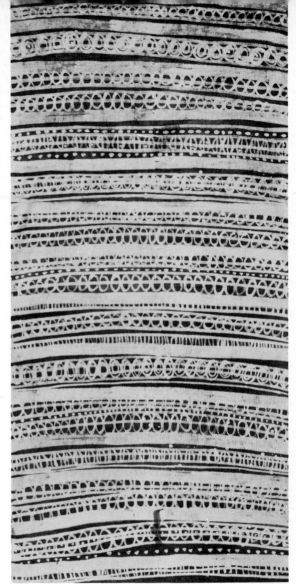

Allover stripe pattern of purple dye on blue fabric by college student

Simple geometric pattern of two colors on white fabric from Jugoslavia

Wall hanging of stylized plant forms, showing crackle effect achieved in final dyeing. By Opal Fleckenstein

Decorative wall hanging by Mary A. Dumas. Courtesy, San Francisco Museum of Art

Wall hanging based on architectural theme. Several dye colors on white cotton. By Sylvia Steiner

Direct Painting of a Batik

Brushing on the first application of wax.
The fabric is placed on waxed paper so
that wax seeping through will not cause
the fabric to stick to the work surface.

The true batik technique which has just been demonstrated (wherein areas are waxed to reserve them and the entire fabric is then dipped into a dye bath) is followed, with modifications from the pure Javanese technique, by most artists working in this medium today. The non-conformist who prefers his own innovations inevitably works out a personal method. No two Western batik artists can be said to approach the medium in exactly the same way. Many of them have experimented with variations on the medium, and several incorporate unorthodox techniques.

One of the common deviations is the hand-painting of the dye onto the unreserved areas, sometimes incorporating this with the dipping procedure. This paint-on technique of applying color to the fabric is a simple exercise which allows for considerable license and gives the beginner an opportunity to experience a variety of possibilities. It is recommended as a first introduction to batik.

One of the advantages of painting on selected reserved areas—rather than dipping the entire fabric in dye for each color—is that several colors may be applied with ease in separated wax-free cloth islands. Colors may also be blended within any one open space. The direct paint-on dyeing technique may be done with strong concentrated dye solution. A simple substitute, though relatively more costly, is waterproof ink. These inks come in a good range of brilliant colors and combine well for intermediate hues. Available in ¾-ounce bottles, they are suggested for small designs, such as silk handkerchiefs. If one is to use them for larger pieces it would be wise to purchase the half-pint, pint, or quart size bottles, as there is a great saving in cost. These inks may be diluted, but for batik purposes full strength is recommended. They are water-soluble in use, but waterproof after they have set. However, they are not guaranteed to be wash-proof and therefore dry cleaning is preferred. One great advantage of these inks is their intermixing quality; a wide range of intermediate hues is possible with them.

In the direct color application, pure colors may be juxtaposed allowing for a brilliance or vibration that super-imposition of colors, commonly used in dipped-dyed batiks, might violate. The process may be continued with waxing and painting for combined colors and details as one develops the design. The final step in the coloring may be the crackling for a linear veined textural effect. This may be done in a bath of dye, as illustrated, but it might also be easily achieved by brushing over the waxed fabric with ink or dye using a wide brush; a 2-inch varnish brush is good for this purpose. Crackling penetrates more if the fabric is immersed in dye. However, to control areas where crackle is desired or to achieve variation in the crackle color in separate parts of the batik, the brush technique is preferable.

A further advantage of the hand-painting approach is that of spontaneity, the ability to build and change certain

Painting selected unreserved areas with colored, waterproof inks. Concentrated dyes may also be used. A variety of colors may be applied in the different isolated islands of the exposed fabric. After this first application of colors, the fabric is allowed to dry.

After a second waxing, which covers parts of the first colors applied, additional colored inks are brushed onto the still exposed areas, creating deeper tones and varied hues.

areas as the design develops, and to constantly work, as the painter does, with changing relationships and adjustments as the image emerges. The completely preconceived work, traced from a carefully done sketch, might very easily end up with a tight sterile end product. The vitality of most works of art results in part from the momentary decisions as well as the deliberations of the artist as he changes the work in progress. The strength of the color, the length it remains in the dye, the number of layers of ink applied, all these sensitive small adjustments are what make the work of art the product of a creative person. Between making the sketch and completing the work the artist inevitably grows; so

must the work. Do not attempt to make a batik look exactly like a pencil drawing, or watercolor, or a cut paper color sketch which you may use for the plan. Do not try to translate an oil painting into the batik technique. The medium does not lend itself to this kind of reproduction with any degree of success. Evolve a style which expresses the medium. This will come if you approach batik freshly and experimentally. Do several tests or samples of the basic steps; wax in lines, or areas, dye or brush color onto the test piece, add more wax, add another color. If the result is a brilliant new color you are already well on your way. If it is a disappointing muddy tone, you have learned something about color. After

several sample runs you are ready to experiment with your first piece. Trying the hand-painted technique might be the quickest way to learn.

To proceed, follow the accompanying sequence of illustrations of a work in progress. The example illustrated was done in greens, blues, and purple on a turquoise colored fabric. After first wax reserving, yellow waterproof ink was used to create a rich green color. After further waxing and coloring with additions of darker green, blue, and purple inks, a wide range of closely related hues was achieved. Final treatment of crackle and a dye bath in dark purple was the only step in which the entire fabric was immersed in dye.

To prepare for a unifying, allover crackle effect, the entire surface of the fabric is covered with wax. After the wax has been cooled to make it more brittle (this can be hastened by placing the waxed fabric in the refrigerator), the fabric is crumpled.

Continue adding wax and painting in with darker colors until the design is completed. This illustration shows the finished design, with the wax removed, before the final treatment for crackle effect.

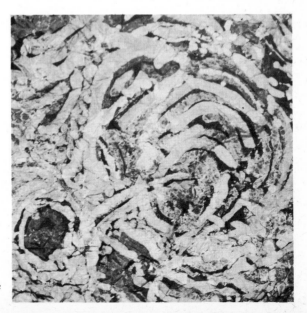

How the crackled wax looks before the final dyeing.

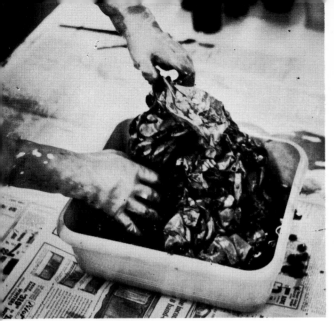

Dipping the fabric in a dark dye bath. The dye penetrates the fabric where the cracked wax exposes it to create an overall pattern of dark veined lines.

Removing wax by rubbing the dried fabric. This wax may be saved for future use.

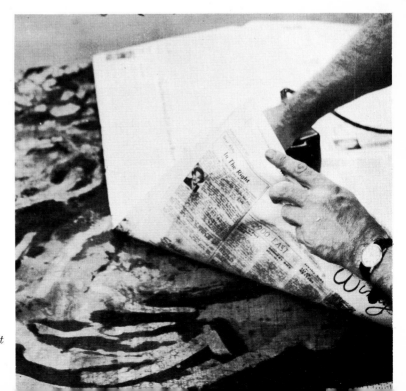

The remaining wax is removed by pressing the fabric with a hot iron. The fabric is protected by layers of newsprint or newspaper to absorb the wax.

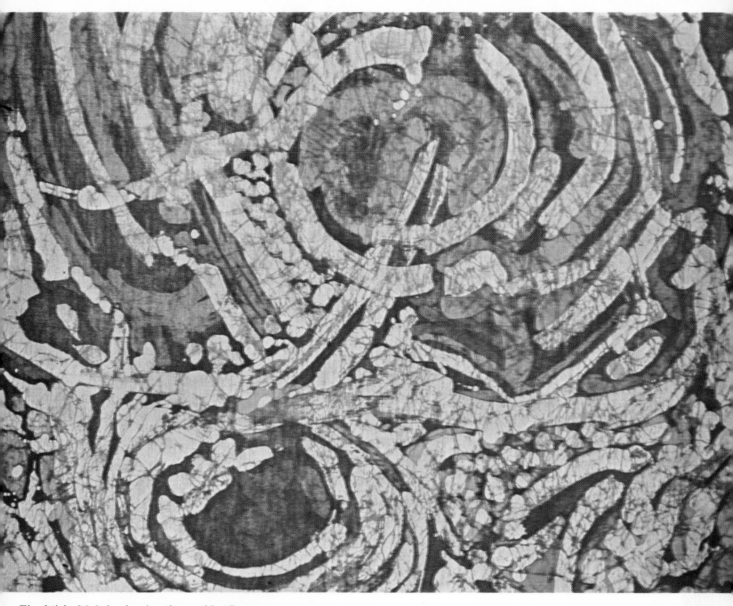

The finished fabric, showing the crackle effect.

*Celebration banner waxed and brush
dyed by a five-year-old. Lettering was
done by the child's father.
Courtesy, Prof. Maurice Grossman
Photo: Balestrero*

*Detail of batik on unbleached muslin by
college student.
EWSC News Bureau*

Using the Tjanting

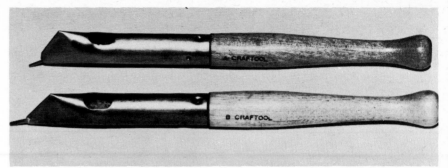

Commercial tjantings available from Craftools, Inc., Woodridge, New Jersey. These tjantings came in three spout sizes: A (the smallest), B, and C.

Until very recently American batik artists were limited to brush techniques and unable to do the fine, controlled line drawing possible with the tjanting, unless they had inherited the tool from someone who had used it in the early 1900's—the period of batik's last great vogue in Europe and the United States.

Handmade tjantings, though simple in concept, require the skill of a fine metal craftsmen for their construction. Shaping the cup, soldering the tube spout to it, and fashioning a handle with which to hold the hot tool require more than amateur ability. Fortunately, however, the tool is now produced commercially. Craftools, Inc., of Woodridge, New Jersey, manufactures three sizes of tjantings which may be obtained directly from the company or found in many well-equipped art supply stores.

The tjanting is used as a drawing tool, depositing hot wax from the metal bowl through a thin tubular spout. The tool is loaded by dipping it into a pan of hot wax and filling the bowl half full. A few practice strokes should be made before waxing the fabric to get a consistent flow of wax. Very hot wax right out of the pan may flow too freely at first. When the wax becomes too sluggish during use, it may be reheated to the proper consistency by holding the bowl of the tjanting over an alcohol lamp. Avoid using a candle flame, since great care must be taken not to carbonize the wax or deposit soot on the spout. Soot smudges are hard to remove from fabrics.

The tjanting is used for lines, for detailing, and for controlled outlining of areas to be broadly filled in by the faster, though cruder, technique of applying wax with a brush. With a little practice

Simple one-color batik with white lines hand drawn with the tjanting, by Michael O'Connell. Courtesy, American Craftsmens Council

and control, the batiker is able to deposit regular lines of wax by barely touching the cloth with the tip of the spout.

The commercial tjantings may be inadequate for the craftsman interested in a wider range of effects. However, once he has become familiar with the potentials and limitations inherent in the tjanting, any craftsman could design his own to suit his particular needs. Designs could be taken to a skilled metal worker who could fabricate tjantings from copper and copper tubing.

"Composition," wall hanging by Maud Rydin. The light lines and dots were laid in wax using a tjanting. The heavier black lines are edges of areas waxed to resist the darkest dye used. They were left exposed to the action of the dye.

Here the tjanting has been combined with brush application. The lightest dots and dashes were waxed before the first dyeing, the darker ones after subsequent dyeings.
Photo by Allen Deyo

Wax resist lines drawn with the tjanting may be handsomely contrasted with lines scratched through wax. Here the artist uses a screwdriver as a scratching tool, taking care not to gouge and tear the fabric. Awls, mimeograph stencil tools, dental instruments, and other pointed, but not sharp, tools are also suitable.
Photo by A. Malmberg

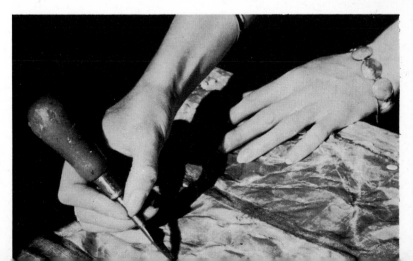

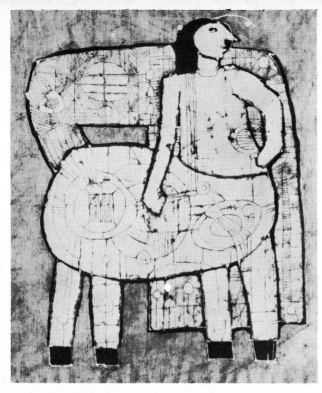

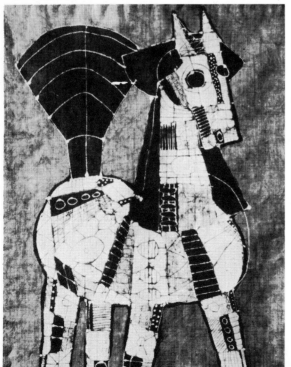

"Centaur," "Birds," and "Horse" by
Maud Rydin. A variety of lines, dots, and
details has been developed with the
tjanting and by scratching through wax.
The bold, large areas contrast with the
delicate, spidery lines. There are two
kinds of lines: the controlled ones
developed with the tjanting and by
scratching and the accidental ones
characteristic of crackling.
Photos by A. Malmberg

Paper Batik

Batik is an extremely versatile technique. Once the basic principle—that certain media will repel other media—is understood, it may be utilized in an infinite variety of ways. One of the most rewarding applications of the resist technique is paper batik. It is simple and inexpensive to do and produces exciting results with a wide range of effects. Paper batik is within the range of the very young child, yet it is also a legitimate graphic technique important to the mature artist. Some unusual contemporary drawings, illustrations, and advertising art incorporate aspects of the resist techniques described here.

The steps for making paper batiks are similar to those for making cloth batiks, the main difference being that the papers are generally not immersed in dye baths. In paper batik the resist is usually brushed or drawn on the paper and covered with another medium, which either rolls off or is scraped or washed off the resist.

Before beginning any extensive project involving much time, it is highly recommended that you experiment with your materials on paper. Paper batik materials, like any others, have their potentials and limitations. A few preliminary exercises in applying the resist and developing dye application techniques will help you discover these and set your goals accordingly.

An important consideration in paper batik is choosing the right kind of paper for the texture or effect you wish to achieve. Although most kinds of paper are suitable, some are not because they are structurally weak. Since the batik process subjects paper to considerable wear, only the sturdier papers should be used. Newsprint, although one of the most popular and available of all papers, should not be used because it will not withstand hard rubbing with crayon or wax. It is therefore especially difficult to control, particularly by young children. Beginners of any age should avoid fragile papers, such as art tissue, as they require unusual care throughout the batik process.

Mimeograph bond and similar papers are recommended for basic experiments. Construction paper, which is quite sturdy, stands up well under repeated rubbing, scrubbing, and wetting. Bristol and poster boards are good when smooth surfaces are desired, and they are easy to work on. For variations in texture, charcoal and rough watercolor paper are particularly rewarding. The "tooth" of these papers holds both resist and dye media well, and promotes interesting application techniques. The wide variety of elegant Oriental papers is suited to both modern and traditional approaches to batiking. Because these papers are interlaced with straw or silk fibers, they stand up well under rough treatment and are particularly suitable for crackling effects.

The color of the paper affects the appearance of the finished work, no matter what resist or coloring media are used over it. For the beginner white paper is suggested. Its surface acts as a reflector for the translucent crayons and gives a brilliance of contrast not possible with colored papers. Colored papers, on the other hand, may be used to create unexpected color mixtures and subtleties which are desirable when brilliance or strong contrast are not the most important aspects of the work. For example, yellow crayon on white paper is sunny and luminescent; the same crayon on blue paper achieves a greenish hue and a duller effect. Generally, light colored crayons that appear bright and clear against white are likely to be muddy and drab on colored grounds.

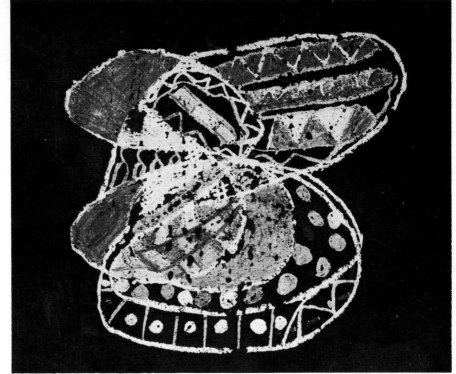

*This first grader used a variety of
colored crayons on white paper, which
were washed over with a thinned solution
of black poster paint.
Photo by Peter Balestrero*

The paper batik technique that most closely resembles fabric batiking is roll-off. In roll-off, the design is applied in wax, and the dye or pigment brushed or dabbed over the paper. The coloring medium will be resisted by the wax and roll off to stain only the unwaxed parts of the paper. Like fabric batiking, roll-off allows a great deal of versatility and uniqueness in approach. The artist may build up his paper batik in various stages by separate waxing and dyeing, or he may combine the numerous kinds and colors of resist media and set them off by a single dyeing.

The most successful and easy to use roll-off resist media are crayon and paraffin. Crayons come in a wide variety of kinds, colors, and sizes, and a bit of experimentation is necessary to determine which are the most successful as resist media. Generally, the most effective crayons are the waxiest. Since a heavy application involving considerable amounts of crayon is necessary—unless one is doing a finely detailed linear work—large kindergarten crayons are recommended. These are cheap and cover well. The recently developed oil crayons, which are more expensive than the kindergarten crayons, blend easily into a wide variety of colors and effects and will prove particularly rewarding for the mature artist. Pressed crayons do not work well as resists. They are too hard and do not deposit as waxy a residue as do the softer crayons and oil crayons.

Paraffin is an excellent and inexpensive resist material, if a colored resist is not desired. It may be used in block form like a crayon or melted and brushed on, as in fabric batiking. Candle stumps may also be used and are easier to handle than a block of paraffin. Either paraffin or candles on colored paper will protect the original color of the paper and allow it to show through the dye media. Melted paraffin will penetrate thin papers and protect both sides, permitting immersion in a dye bath for the crackle effect. Since paraffin or candles serve little purpose in most finished batiks, the medium may be removed by placing the batik between newsprint or other absorbent papers and pressing it with a warm iron. Sometimes, however, the strength and luminosity that the wax gives is quite desirable in a finished work. For a translucent panel, such as a shoji screen, the wax-impregnated papers are very effective.

After the waxed lines or areas are put down, the dye media are applied. These media may be watercolors, inks, fabric dyes, or tempera paints. Watercolors, fabric dyes, and colored inks are transparent and easily roll off waxed areas. Tempera, or poster, paints must be thinned; otherwise the pigment particles and the binders used in the paints tend to cover the wax design. If adequately thinned and quickly applied, tempera rolls off easily too.

An important aspect in applying the paint or dye is the way in which you brush it on. All media should be applied with soft watercolor brushes, pointed ones for details and broad flat ones for washes. Avoid stiff bristle brushes, since they are likely to scratch through the resist. Work quickly and smoothly with little stroking or rubbing back and forth. The more you scrub with the brush, the more likely the paint will cover the resist.

A fanciful landscape of trees created by
a six-year-old using colored wax crayons
with a watercolor wash.
Photo by Peter Balestrero

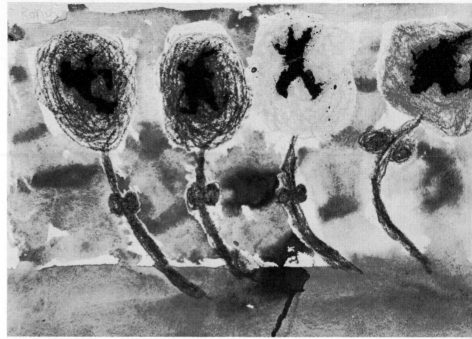

Sun rising on an Indian encampment by a
junior high school student (7th grade).
The multicolored crayon drawing on
white paper was covered with a black and
a blue-green watercolor wash.
Courtesy, Tucson Public Schools
Photo by Peter Balestrero

A simple, direct statement in crayon resist. The multi-colored design of wax crayons was boldly applied to white paper. Then the entire surface was covered with black poster paint, which rolled off the waxed areas, texturing them somewhat with small spots of paint. Rosemarie Mandarino, The Studio, Binney and Smith, Inc.

The train switchyard by a third-grade student. A red watercolor wash was brushed over the blue, yellow, and black crayon drawing.
Photo by Peter Balestrero

Color was applied to white paper with soft oil crayons and blended by smearing. Black watercolor was then brushed on in selected areas to silhouette the forms. Much of the white paper is left exposed.

The roll-off technique using oil crayons. The drawing was made with yellow, green, and orange crayons on white paper. Washes of blue and black watercolor were applied in controlled areas to achieve a combined resist and watercolor quality.

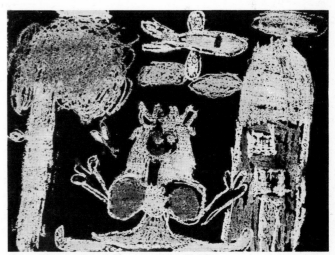

Crayon resist by a seven-year-old. Boldly applied crayon in several colors was covered with thinned opaque black watercolor, which rolled off the waxed areas.

The star was first drawn in pencil on white paper. The shapes were colored with wax crayons and paraffin (to permit the white paper to show through). A blue wash was brushed over the design.

A geometric repeat pattern in crayons with a black watercolor wash. Courtesy, Prang Textile Studio, American Crayon Company

Instead of drawing with crayons, the artist brushed melted wax over the paper before applying a dark watercolor wash.

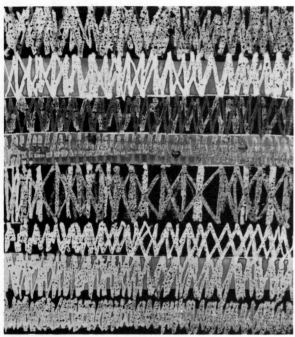

Stripe designs in multi-colored crayons over colored paper. A wash of blue watercolor was brushed over certain areas, black over others.

Wax resist drawing works well for creating high lights or modeling a form. To create this portrait, white crayon was applied to colored construction paper. Black watercolor wash was brushed over the crayon.

Rubbings involve transferring a surface texture onto paper. This is done by placing the paper over the textured object and lightly and repeatedly rubbing until the pattern of the texture appears. The more prominent parts of the texture will receive more rubbing and emerge as the most dominant parts of the pattern. Rubbings may be easily made with crayons or paraffin, and are greatly enhanced by the batik technique.

Rubbings may be made from kitchen gadgets, grainy wood, leaves, perforated metals, bas reliefs, and other man-made or natural items. Anything whose texture forms an interesting pattern may be used, as long as the texture has definite contrast.

Only light, strong, fairly flexible papers should be used in making a rubbing. Oriental papers are ideal, but good quality rag content paper will do as well. Thick stiff papers will not follow the contours of the texture, and no definite image can be produced. The crayon or paraffin must be carefully applied, broadside not point-end. Work gently, for rough textured objects are likely to tear the paper if you rub too roughly. While rubbing, keep the paper and object steady. If either moves, the image will be blurred or smeared, rather than sharp and clear.

Rubbings made from veined leaves and a collapsible metal vegetable basket. The impression is created by placing fairly thin paper over the textured object and rubbing crayons or uncolored wax over it. The black watercolor wash which was applied to the paper rolled off the waxed impression.

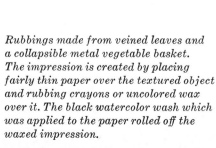

A black India ink drawing was made on heavy tracing paper. Crayons in a variety of colors were used to fill in the figures and the background. The entire surface was then covered with a wash of black poster paint. The crayon areas were uncovered by scraping through the wash and rubbed for added luster.
Alexandra Henn, The Studio, Binney and Smith, Inc.

Over an India ink drawing on heavy tracing paper, the artist applied flat areas with colored wax crayons. A textured effect was achieved by placing the paper over wire screening and veined leaves. The entire surface was covered with a wash of black poster paint. Finally, the surface was scraped to reveal the crayon and burnished with a wad of cotton.
Rosemarie Mandarino, The Studio, Binney and Smith, Inc.

Scrape-off

For strong contrast between waxed and dyed areas, undiluted poster paints or India ink may be used. These media, however, do not roll off the wax. They stick and obliterate the image. Therefore, after they have dried, they must be scraped off the waxed areas.

If you plan to use the scraping technique, make sure you apply enough crayon or paraffin to the paper so that you won't scrape straight through to the paper. Scraping is particularly effective on rough-textured papers. With a razor blade you may skim over the most prominent parts of the paper, and leave interesting little valleys of paint or ink. When the scraping technique is used on smooth papers, the result resembles a block print. In fact, some artists who work in block printing make preliminary sketches with this resist technique.

Wash-off techniques are variations of the classical paste resist on fabric explained in Chapter I. In both modern and classical methods, a water soluble resist is covered by a non-water soluble dye or other coloring agent. This dye covers both paper or fabric and resist, but penetrates only the former. When the waterproof agent has set, the resist is washed off with water.

Modern wash-off paste resists include library paste, wheat paste, flour pastes, and corn starch. Poster paint, undiluted, is quite effective and appropriate for school use. Gum arabic applied the thickness of heavy cream will give unusual effects. These resists may be used by themselves or in combination with other water-soluble resists.

The steps in all wash-off resist methods are similar. First the water-soluble resist is applied quite thick. It should almost form little mounds on the paper. After it has dried, waterproof inks are carefully brushed on. Care should be taken not to rub these back and forth over the resist, as the resist may smear or run. Allow the ink to penetrate completely the fibers of the paper, dry, and set. After it has set, gently wash away the resist. Do not scrub the paper; it isn't necessary.

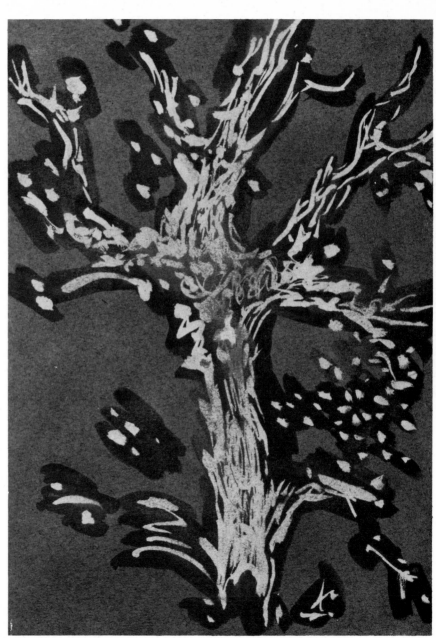

White poster paint was applied in a thick paste consistency to colored construction paper. When it was thoroughly dry, waterproof color was brushed over it in selected areas of the composition. When the color was dry, the entire painting was washed under the tap. The color washed off the thickly painted white areas.

Several kinds of substances may be applied to paper, painted over, and then picked up, leaving unpainted the areas they formerly covered. These resist materials fall into two broad categories—liquid adherents and masking papers.

The best liquid resist for the rub-off technique is rubber cement. Rubber cement may be brushed, dripped from the container, or dripped from the brush in much the same way as the action painter dribbles oil paint onto his canvas. This medium and its method of application do not allow the control possible with other resist techniques. However, exciting accidental results and a spontaneous quality can produce very handsome works.

When the rubber cement has dried, watercolor, thinned poster paint, or inks may be applied over it. The cement will resist the colors, which will penetrate only the uncovered areas. After the paints or inks have dried, the cement may be removed by rubbing it off with the fingers.

Masking papers include frisket paper and gummed papers and masking tapes. These are temporarily stuck onto paper and later removed by peeling them off. Since both papers and tapes must be cut to shape, very little free-form design or accidental effects will result. The use of these materials must be deliberate and well planned. The most effective application of masking papers is probably in advertising art. Letters, words, symbols, simple geometric forms, and large areas may be reserved.

High quality, hard finish papers must be used for both rubber cement and masking papers in the rub-off technique. Soft, fibrous, or fuzzy papers will tear up with the resist materials when they are removed. Rubber cement may be used on good bond paper; gummed papers and tapes should always be used on very heavy papers or on boards.

These examples show the distinct character of the flow of the rubber cement. The thin cement is applied by dripping from the brush or brushing directly on the paper. When it is dry, watercolor or ink can be brushed over it. After the color wash has dried, the cement is rubbed off, leaving exposed the paper it had covered.

GALLERY OF EXAMPLES/TRADITIONAL BATIKS

*Adire cloth, an example
of Indigo paste resist
fabric from Nigeria.
Courtesy, Art Department,
Ohio University*

Traditional paste resist
batik design from China.

Stencil print batik for
Kimono from Japan.

Javanese Wayang figure.
(Collection of the author.)

Batik from India,
incorporating writing and
figurative designs in a
lively overall pattern.
Courtesy, Standard Oil Co.
(N.J.)

Tulis batik, hand waxed with the tjanting, from Java.
Photo: Archives of the Kon Inst. v/d Tropen

Parang Rusak selen batik design from Java. Courtesy, Republic of Indonesia

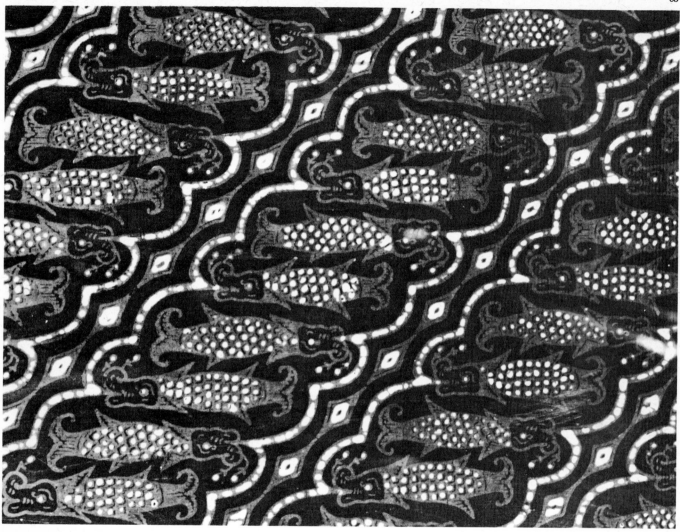

Oldest known form of
batik, a single color
ketan-rice (paste) resist.
The paste was probably
applied with a bamboo
stick or the fingers. The
edges of the figures are
not sharply defined,
probably because of the
coarse weave of the
fabric and the means of
application.
Photo: Archives of the
Kon Inst. v/d Tropen

Parang Kusumo (fish
variation) batik pattern
from Java.
Courtesy,
Republic of Indonesia

Parang Klitik Garuda
design of Java, showing
the sun bird of Hindu
mythology. A traditional
pattern to be worn only
by the sultans.
Courtesy,
Standard Oil Co. (N.J.)

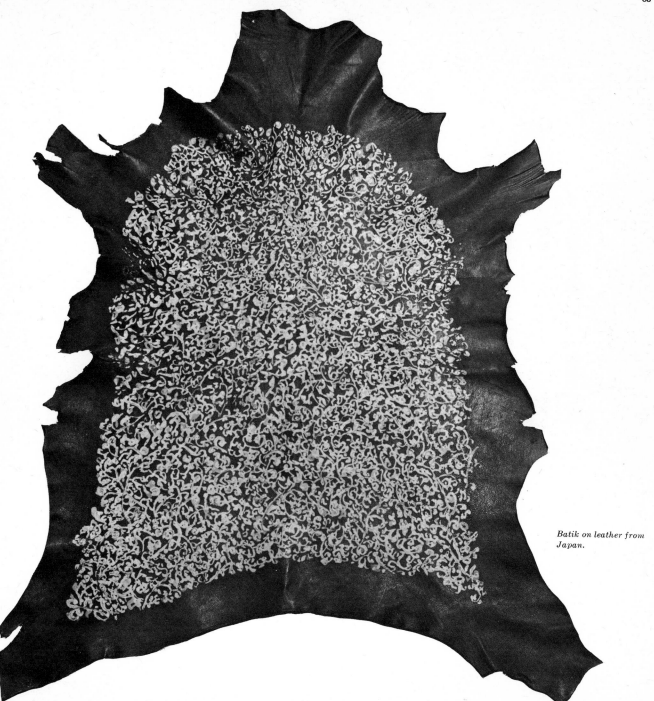

Batik on leather from Japan.

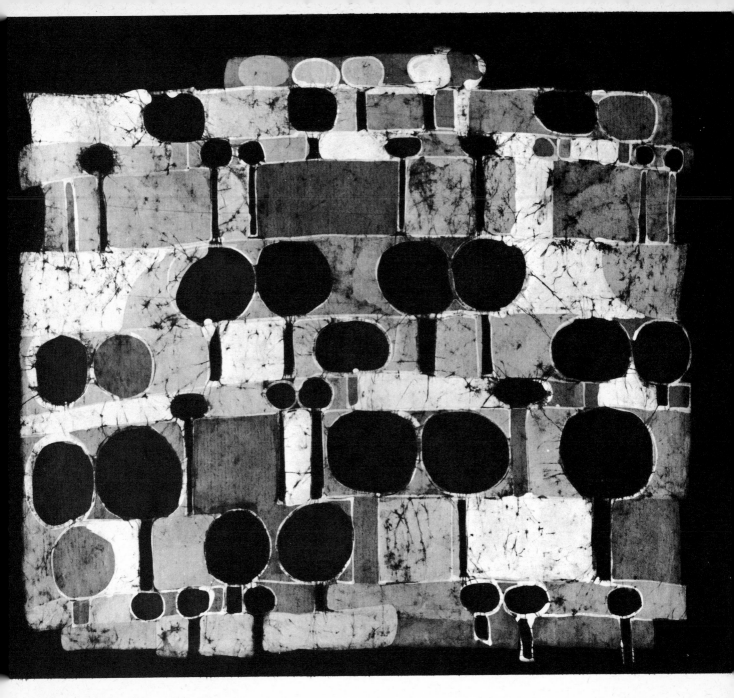

Wall hanging of a garden, showing decorative stylization of trees and grass, by Sylvia Steiner. Several colors on white cotton.

CONTEMPORARY BATIKS

Many contemporary artists and designers
are exploring the medium of batik with
great satisfaction and success. Although
the approaches differ and each artist
expresses his unique stamp, all the works
illustrated here show batik as a fine
technique for contemporary graphic art
as applied to textiles.

The artists whose works appear in the
following pages have achieved recognition
in the field and their different styles are
easily discernible. By comparing several
works of one artist the reader is able
to observe that artist's special treatment
of the medium.

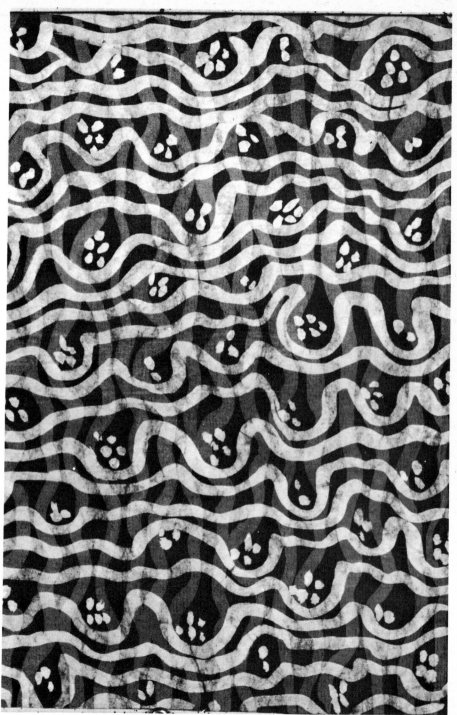

*Two-color design on white
fabric from Jugoslavia,
showing spontaneous use
of the brush in waxing.*

"Island City" by Joseph Almyda. An architectural theme conceived in flat, geometric patterns using several colors on white fabric.

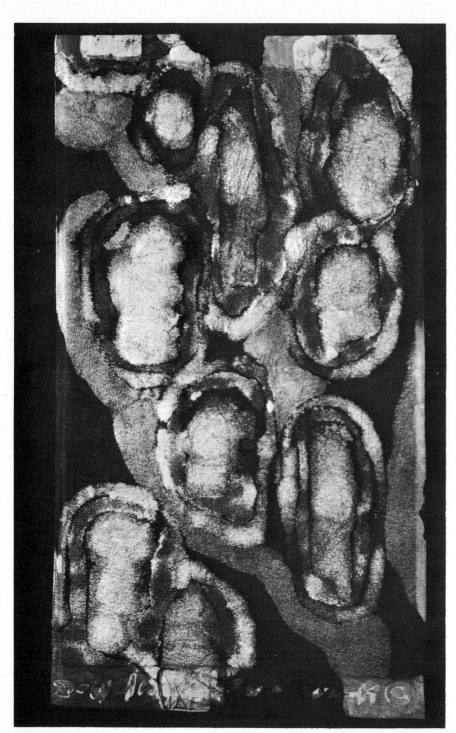

*Batik on terry cloth
(20″ x 40″) by Opal
Fleckenstein. The texture
of the fabric gives a rich
effect to the dyed areas.
The three dye colors are
orange, red, and deep
brown on white.
Photo by Peter Balestrero*

72

*"Peaceable Kingdom"
(66" by 44") by Vaki.
Colors: greens, blues &
golds.*

This richly textured batik by Ed Stachofsky was achieved by combining the techniques of batik and tie and dye on Turkish toweling.
EWSC News Bureau Photo

Detail of freely brushed design by Elenita Brown. (Photo by Joey Starr.)

"Sunburst," (30" x 30") by Adrienne Kraut. A three-dye batik using yellow ochre, orange, and brown on white fabric. Photo by Peter Balestrero

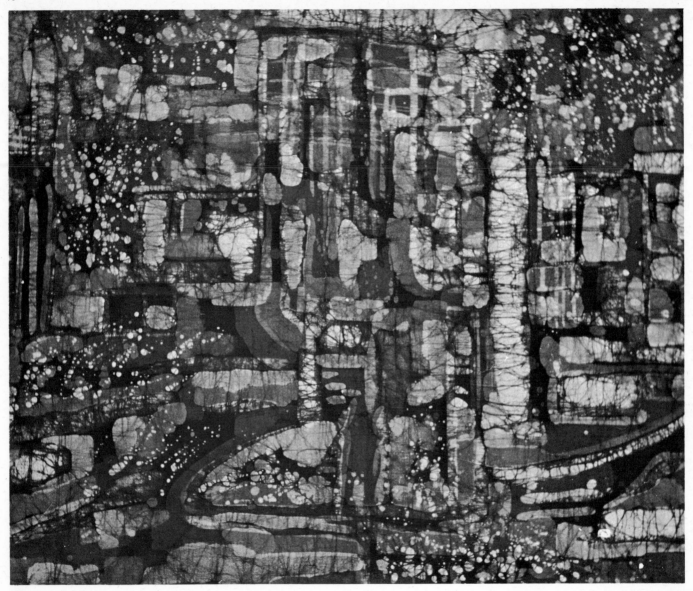

"The Lights of Denver"
(65" x 30") by Opal
Fleckenstein. (EWSC
News Bureau Photo.)

*"Ancient Ruins" by
Adrienne Kraut. Painted
with several sizes of soft
and stiff bristle brushes.*

*Batik with appliqué by
Jodi Robbin.*

*Opposite Page
Detail of batik by
Elenita Brown.*

"Mechanical Mass" (5 feet by 4 feet) by John W. Mulder. Batik on brown silk in green, yellow, white, black, and pink. (Photo by William Eng.)

Detail of a wall hanging by Mary A. Dumas. The subtle value contrast created by several dye colors on white fabric produces the effect of low relief.
Courtesy, American Craftsmen's Council

82

Batik on burlap
(28″ x 40″) by Opal
Fleckenstein. The design
is the result of two
dyeings, green and brown,
on the tan fabric. The
burlap required waxing
on both sides.
Photo by Peter Balestrero

Figurative batik by Barbara Bernard, Junior high school student. (Courtesy San Diego City Schools.)

"Water Hole" (6 feet by 3 feet) by John W. Mulder. Batik on silk in beige, yellow, orange, and brown. (Photo by William Eng.)

"Totem," detail of a silk wall hanging by Helen Frick Jones. The black lines were left exposed for the final, darkest dyeing. Brush marks left by the waxing are easily observed.

Batik in Interior Design

The batiks on the following four pages
were designed for the production of
repeat patterns for draperies, upholstery,
and fashion.

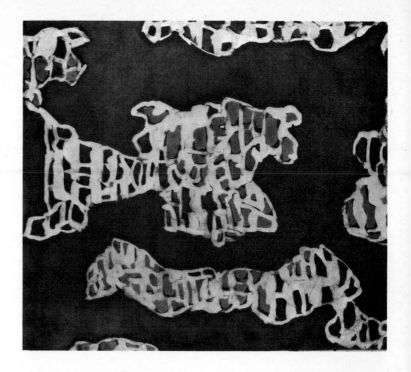

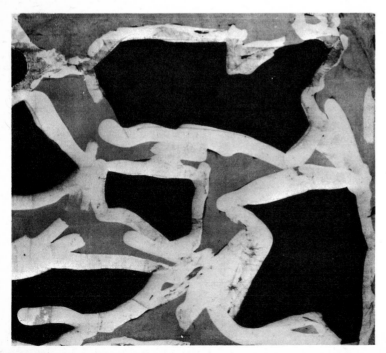

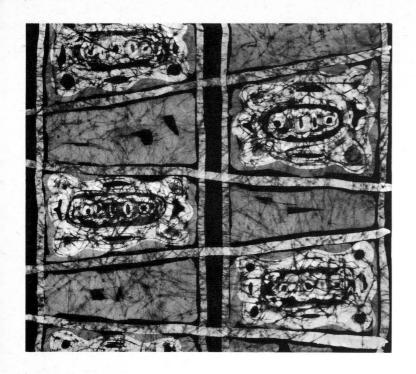

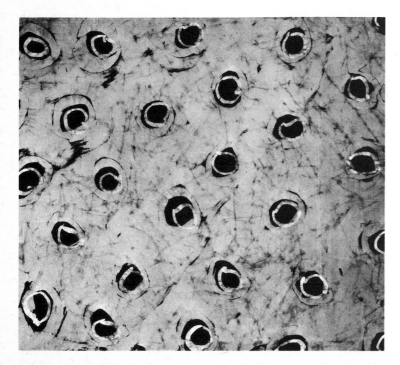

The batik technique used
to decorate Easter eggs.
These are examples of
traditional pysanky
Ukranian Easter eggs,
showing the variety of
symmetrical designs used;
no two pysanky eggs are
ever identical. Only
uncooked eggs, washed in
a warm solution of water
and vinegar, are suitable.
Wax should be applied
with a thin brush or a
tjanting. The eggs can be
dyed in ordinary household
or Easter egg dyes. Each
darker value is achieved
by a progressive reserving
and dyeing.